WORKBOOK

FOR

Disconnected Kids

A Practical Guide On The Groundbreaking Brain Balance Program for Children with Autism, ADHD, Dyslexia, and Other Neurological Disorders

HEATH PRINT

TABLE OF CONTENT

HOW TO USE THE WORKBOOK

Welcome! You got here, which means you chose right. This is a companion book for "Disconnected Kids: The Groundbreaking Brain Balance Program for Children with Autism, ADHD, Dyslexia, and Other Neurological Disorders" by Dr. Robert Melillo. This Workbook has been well crafted to enhance your understanding and help you use the Original book to the very best. Never miss a point and digest every single detail; this is what this workbook offers. Now, let me put you through how to make the most of this workbook.

Step 1: Chapter Overviews and Summaries

Before diving into the core lessons and self-introspection questions, begin with the chapter overviews and summaries. These sections are designed to give you a concise recap of the main points from each chapter of the original book. Use these summaries as a refresher or to gain clarity on the key concepts discussed by Dr. Melillo.

Step 2: Key Lessons

Each chapter summary is followed by core lessons derived from the chapter's content. These lessons distill the essence of what Dr. Melillo is teaching into practical, actionable insights. Pay close attention to these lessons, as they will be crucial for applying the Brain Balance Program's principles in real-life scenarios.

Step 3: Self-Reflection Questions

Following the core lessons, you'll find self-introspection questions. These questions are designed to prompt deep thinking and personal reflection about how the chapter's content applies to you and your child's unique situation. Answering these questions honestly will help you internalize the lessons and prepare you for effective application.

Step 4: Applying What You've Learned

As you progress through the workbook, begin to apply what you've learned to your daily life. This might involve modifying your approach to your child's challenges, trying new activities, or adjusting your expectations. The real value of this workbook lies in its application, so don't hesitate to put theory into practice.

Step 5: Self-Evaluation Questions

At the end of the workbook, you'll find a section titled "SELF EVALUATION QUESTIONS." This section is designed to help you reflect on your journey through the workbook and assess your progress. These questions will guide you in evaluating the effectiveness of the strategies you've implemented and identify areas for continued growth and learning.

Additional Tips:

Take Your Time: Don't rush through the workbook. Take the time to thoroughly digest each section before moving on to the next.

Take Notes: Feel free to jot down additional thoughts, observations, or questions that arise as you work through the material.

Revisit Often: Your understanding and application of the Brain Balance Program will evolve over time. Revisiting sections of this workbook periodically can provide new insights and reinforce your learning.

By following these steps and engaging deeply with the content of this workbook, you're setting yourself and your child up for success.

Remember, this journey is a marathon, not a sprint. Be patient, stay committed, and watch as the principles of the Brain Balance Program transform your child's life.

SUMMARY/OVERVIEW

"Disconnected Kids: The Groundbreaking Brain Balance Program for Children with Autism, ADHD, Dyslexia, and Other Neurological Disorders" by Dr. Robert Melillo is a comprehensive guide that offers a beacon of hope to parents and caregivers of children with various neurological disorders. This book delves into the heart of how imbalances in the brain's functioning can lead to the symptoms associated with conditions like autism, ADHD, dyslexia, and more. Dr. Melillo's work is not just another academic treatise; it's a practical roadmap designed to navigate the complexities of neurological disorders, offering effective strategies for intervention and improvement.

At its core, "Disconnected Kids" introduces readers to the Brain Balance Program, an integrative approach that combines physical exercises, dietary changes, and cognitive training to address and correct imbalances in the brain. Dr. Melillo's thesis is built on the foundation that many neurological disorders arise from a disparity in the communication between the brain's hemispheres. This groundbreaking perspective shifts the focus from treating symptoms to targeting the root cause of these conditions.

The book is meticulously structured, beginning with an enlightening overview of the rise in neurological disorders among children. Dr. Melillo lays out startling statistics that frame the urgency of addressing this "major health threat." He provides a historical context that illustrates how perceptions of these disorders have evolved, shedding light on the increasing prevalence of diagnoses and the impact on families and society at large.

Following this introduction, Dr. Melillo delves into the scientific basis of the Brain Balance Program. He articulates a compelling argument for the interconnectedness of the brain's physical structure with cognitive functions and behaviors. The explanation of how imbalances between the brain's hemispheres can manifest in various disorders is both accessible and enlightening. This section of the book is crucial for understanding the rationale behind the program's approach to treatment.

The subsequent chapters are dedicated to the practical application of the Brain Balance Program. Dr. Melillo breaks down the program into manageable components, detailing exercises, dietary guidelines, and cognitive activities designed to harmonize brain function. What sets this book apart is its holistic approach; it recognizes the importance of a supportive environment and the role of family in the healing process. The program is not presented as a quick fix but as a commitment to a lifestyle change that fosters optimal brain development and function.

Perhaps the most impactful aspect of "Disconnected Kids" is the emphasis on hope and empowerment. Dr. Melillo provides case studies and testimonials that offer real-world evidence of the program's success. These stories resonate with emotional depth, illustrating the transformative impact on families who have navigated the challenges of neurological disorders.

In conclusion, "Disconnected Kids" is more than just a book; it's a comprehensive guide for parents and caregivers seeking to understand and improve the lives of children with neurological disorders. Dr. Melillo's Brain Balance Program presents a revolutionary approach that challenges conventional wisdom and offers a path to a brighter future. By addressing the underlying brain imbalances, the program opens the door to achieving remarkable progress, making "Disconnected Kids" an indispensable resource for anyone touched by these conditions.

DIFFERENT SYMPTOMS, ONE PROBLEM

Understanding the Minds of Disconnected Kids

Key Lessons

1. **Unified Origin of Diverse Illnesses:** Despite their disparate symptoms and diagnoses, many neurological disorders in children, such as autism, ADHD, dyslexia, and others, are caused by similar underlying imbalances in brain development and function. This similar origin indicates that brain balancing therapies might improve a wide range of disorders.

2. **Neurological disorders are rapidly increasing.** The enormous increase of childhood neurological abnormalities in recent decades implies that these are not isolated difficulties, but rather part of a larger, growing trend. This surge emphasizes the critical importance of raising awareness, understanding, and taking action to combat brain-based illnesses.

3. **Effects of Early Diagnosis and Intervention**: Early detection and intervention in neurological illnesses has the potential to drastically change a child's developmental trajectory. Understanding the signs and seeking treatment quickly can lead

4. **Holistic Strategy to Treatment:** Treating neurological illnesses necessitates a diverse approach that extends beyond medicine or single therapy. Integrating physical, cognitive,

and nutritional measures based on individual needs can enhance brain balance and improve overall performance.

5. **The Role of Environment and Lifestyle:** The environment and lifestyle variables, which range from nutrition and physical exercise to technology exposure and stress, play critical roles in the development and management of neurological illnesses. Creating supportive settings and healthy habits can help to improve brain health and reduce symptoms.

Self-Reflection Questions

1. **Given the common root of many diseases, how do you perceive the link between the symptoms your kid exhibits?**

---

2. Given the fast growth in neurological illnesses, what actions can you do to raise your knowledge and comprehension of these conditions?

----

3. Given the significance of early detection and intervention, have you observed any indicators in your kid that may necessitate further study or contact with a professional?

4. Consider the holistic approach to treatment: what areas (physical, cognitive, and nutritional) could you investigate or improve in your child's care routine to promote brain balance?

5. **Given the importance of environment and lifestyle, what adjustments can you do in your family to promote a healthy lifestyle and environment for your child?**

CHILDREN'S BRAINS REALLY ARE CHANGEABLE

How the Developing Brain Is Wired

Key Lessons

1. **Neuroplasticity in Youngsters: The brain's ability to rearrange itself by generating new neural connections throughout life is particularly evident in children. This ability to alter implies that early intervention and proper therapy can result in considerable improvements in neurological illnesses.**

2. **Critical Growth Periods: Certain forms of learning and development in the brain are best suited to specific periods. Understanding these important stages can help parents and educators give the appropriate stimulation and support to enhance a child's cognitive and emotional development.**

3. **The Role of Environment: A child's brain development is heavily influenced by his or her environment. Positive,**

stimulating settings can improve brain function, whilst negative situations can inhibit it.

4. Brain Hemisphere Integration: Healthy cognitive, social, and emotional growth requires balanced development of the brain's left and right hemispheres. Activities that develop balance can assist youngsters with neurological impairments in improving their abilities.

5. Early Detection and Intervention: The sooner a neurological issue is detected and treated, the better the result for the kid. Early intervention makes use of the brain's plasticity to reduce the impact of abnormalities on a child's development.

Self-Reflection Questions

1. **Neuroplasticity in Children: Consider the settings and activities you give for your child. Are they intended to stimulate and foster new brain connections that can help overcome neurological challenges?**

----

2. **Critical Periods of Development:** Consider whether you are aware of your child's important developmental phases. Have you scheduled their learning and development activities to coincide with these ideal times?

_____

_____

_____

_____

_____

_____

_____

_____

_____

_____

_____

_____

_____

_____

_____

_____

_____

3. **The Role of Environment: Assess the quality of your child's environment. Is it enriching and supportive enough to promote their brain development?**

----

4. **Integration of Brain Hemispheres: Consider your child's activity balance. Do they encourage equal development of the left and right hemispheres of the brain?**

----

5. **Early detection and intervention. Consider how proactive you have been in seeking diagnosis and treatment for any neurological or developmental issues. Have you fully realized the potential benefits of early intervention?**

WHEN THE BRAIN MISBEHAVES

A Left Brain, Right Brain Disconnect

Key Lessons

1. **Understanding Brain Imbalance:** This chapter emphasizes the importance of balance between the left and right hemispheres of the brain in sustaining neurological health. Imbalances can contribute to a variety of neurological problems, including ADHD, dyslexia, and autism.

2. **Recognizing Early Indicators:** Highlights the significance of early identification and acknowledgment of signs of brain imbalance. Early intervention can help to reduce the effects of these diseases on a child's social, intellectual, and personal development.

3. **The Impact of Neurological Problems on Behavior** investigates how neurological disorders caused by brain imbalances might emerge as behavioral, social, or academic dysfunctions, impacting all aspects of a child's life and family.

4. **The Role of Environment and Lifestyle:** Examines how environmental influences and lifestyle choices might impact brain development and function, arguing that

specific treatments can promote brain balance and enhance results.

5. **Empowerment Through Knowledge: Emphasizes the necessity of informing parents, caregivers, and educators on brain imbalances and neurological illnesses. Knowledge enables them to seek out suitable therapies and support mechanisms for afflicted youngsters..**

Self-Reflection Questions

1. **Understanding Brain Imbalance: Are you familiar with the notion of brain imbalance and its possible effects on behavior and learning? Do you see any indicators of a brain imbalance in yourself or someone you know?**

----

2. Recognizing early signs: Have you ever seen any early indicators of neurological diseases in yourself or others? How receptive do you believe you or others have been in addressing these signs?

3. **The Effect of Neurological Disorders on Behavior:** Consider how neurological problems may have impacted your own or someone else's conduct, social relationships, or academic success. Can you point to particular occasions when these impacts were evident?

----

4. **The Importance of Environment and Lifestyle Consider the circumstances and lifestyles that have shaped your life or the lives of those you know. How do you believe these things have impacted brain balance and neurological health?**

----

5. **Empowerment Through Knowledge: How empowered do you feel in seeking out information and treatments for neurological disorders? What measures can you take to further educate yourself or assist someone in need of help?**

RECONNECTING THE BRAIN

The Ten Principles of the Brain Balance Program

Key Lessons

1. Understanding the multidimensional nature of neurological illnesses such as autism, ADHD, and dyslexia necessitates a holistic strategy that treats physical, cognitive, and nutritional elements all at once.

2. Brain Plasticity and Development: Recognizing the brain's ability to adapt and develop at any age, with a focus on specific activities and exercises that help improve neural connections and promote hemispheric balance.

3. Importance of Early Intervention Recognizing the key window for intervention in childhood, when focused activities can greatly influence the brain's developmental trajectory, increasing behavioral, social, and intellectual functioning.

4. Customized Therapeutic Activities: The need to adapt therapeutic activities to each child's unique

requirements, based on a comprehensive assessment of their individual problems and abilities, in order to successfully stimulate brain growth and functional progress.

5. **Integrative Support System:** A supportive environment that incorporates not just therapy interventions, but also family engagement and educational accommodations, resulting in a comprehensive support system that promotes the child's growth and well-being.

Self-Reflection Questions

1. How do you perceive the balance between your brain's hemispheres, and how can you engage in activities that improve neural connection and balance?

2. Based on the idea of brain plasticity, what actions can you do in your everyday life to promote ongoing learning and brain development?

3. Given the significance of early intervention, what indicators or behaviors do you believe suggest the need for more examination or assistance in a child's development?

----

4. In light of the necessity for personalized therapeutic activities, how can you modify your approach to meet a child's specific developmental needs and strengths?

---

5. Consider the integrated support system idea; what steps can you take to create a more supporting and caring environment for the growth of children in your care or community?

_____

_____

_____

_____

_____

_____

_____

_____

_____

_____

_____

_____

_____

_____

_____

_____

MASTER HEMISPHERIC CHECKLIST

Identifying a Left or a Right Brain Deficiency

Key Lessons

1. **Understanding Hemispheric Weaknesses: Recognize that children with neurological diseases such as ADHD, autism, dyslexia, and others may have deficiencies in one hemisphere of the brain over the other. Identifying whether a kid has a left or right brain deficit is critical for developing individualized therapy strategies.**

2. **Signs and symptoms of Left-Brain Deficiency: Learn the major signs of a left-brain shortage, which might include difficulty with reasoning, sequencing, linear thinking, and even language-related impairments. Certain symptoms frequently appear as scholastic difficulties in disciplines that demand these cognitive capacities.**

3. **Signs and symptoms of Right Brain Deficiency:** Recognize the signs of a right brain impairment, which frequently causes difficulties with creativity, spatial awareness, face recognition, and social relationships. Children with right brain impairment may fail to perceive context, interpret social cues, and do activities that require holistic thinking.

4. The importance of early detection: Understand the importance of detecting hemispheric defects early in a child's development. Early discovery allows for more effective therapies, possibly improving academic, social, and behavioral outcomes for children with neurological diseases.

5. Tactics for Supporting Hemispheric Balance: Discover strategies and activities that can help the growth of the less dominant hemisphere, resulting in more balanced brain function. These might include cognitive exercises, physical activities, and therapeutic treatments customized to the child's individual requirements.

Self-Reflection Questions

1. **Understanding Your Child's Challenges: Have you found any trends in your child's behavior or academic performance that suggest a hemisphere deficiency? Consider if these problems are more suited to left or right brain processes.**

----

2. Observing Social and Academic Interaction: Which
   tasks do your child find more difficult in social contexts
   or at homework time? Does this suggest a probable left
   or right brain deficiency?

----

3. **Early detection and intervention. Consider your child's developmental history. Were there early signals of hemispheric imbalance that, in retrospect, may have predicted their present challenges?**

----

4. **Exploring Supportive Strategies: What tactics have you used to help your child's less dominant hemisphere? Consider if they have been beneficial, or whether alternative techniques might provide greater help.**

----

5. **Seeking professional guidance: Have you sought professional help to examine and treat your child's probable hemispheric deficiencies? Consider the actions you've done and whether you need additional or alternative expert advice.**

WHAT TO EXPECT FROM BRAIN BALANCE

How to Interpret the Results You Will Experience

Key Lessons

1. **Understanding Neurological Diversity: Recognize that each child's brain development is unique, and neurological problems appear differently in various children. Because of this variation, the Brain Balance Program's results might vary greatly, stressing tailored methods over one-size-fits-all solutions.**

2. **Expectation Management: Establish reasonable growth goals. Significant changes are feasible, but they must be made gradually and consistently. Understanding this helps to keep you motivated and committed to the program.**

3. **The approach focuses on holistic development, emphasizing the need of treating cognitive, physical, and dietary components of brain health. This comprehensive approach guarantees that improvements are long-lasting and have an influence on many aspects of a child's life.**

4. **The Importance of Early Intervention:** Early diagnosis and intervention can result in more significant and long-lasting changes. Because of the flexibility of the brain in younger children, treatments can be more successful, emphasizing the necessity of prompt action.

5. Success in the Brain Balance Program is assessed in more ways than just academic performance. Changes in social conduct, emotional management, and overall well-being can be used to track improvement.

Self-Reflection Questions

1. How do you presently see neurological variety, and how can this affect your approach to the Brain Balance Program?

----

2. What are your particular goals for progressing through the Brain Balance Program, and how do you intend to track and celebrate these successes over time?

---

3. How are you prepared to support holistic growth, including cognitive, physical, and dietary adjustments, to ensure the Brain Balance Program's success?

----

4. Reflecting on the need of early intervention, how quickly do you respond to concerns about neurological development, and what actions can you take to provide timely support?

5. Beyond academic performance, what improvements in social conduct, emotional control, and overall well-being do you want to witness, and how will you assess their success?

HEMISPHERIC HOME SENSORY-MOTOR ASSESSMENT

How to Detect a Left or a Right Brain Deficiency

Key Lessons

1. **Understanding Brain Imbalances: Recognizing that behavioral, social, or scholastic difficulties can sometimes be caused by imbalances between the brain's hemispheres is critical for determining the underlying causes of neurological problems.**

2. **Identifying Symptoms of Hemispheric Deficiency: Learning to recognize particular symptoms associated with left or right brain impairments can help parents and educators provide more focused solutions.**

3. **The Function of Sensory-Motor Activities Sensory-motor exercises play an important role in brain development and, when used appropriately, can assist to balance hemispheric deficits.**

4. **Assessment Procedures: Learning basic, home-based assessment techniques can help parents and caregivers**

recognize potential brain imbalances and initiate early intervention.

5. **Customized Intervention Techniques:** Creating personalized intervention strategies based on the unique hemisphere insufficiency can result in more successful outcomes when treating and helping children with neurological diseases.

Self-Reflection Questions

1. Have you seen any behaviors in your kid that may suggest a hemispheric imbalance, and how do these observations relate to known signs of left or right brain deficiencies?

----

2. What sensory-motor exercises are you aware of that might help your child develop their or her less dominant hemisphere?

----

3. How comfortable are you with completing home-based evaluations to discover potential brain imbalances, and what extra knowledge or resources may you require to do so effectively?

----

4. Given the treatments you are already aware of, how may they be customized to target specific hemisphere gaps more effectively?

---

5. Given the growing frequency of neurological problems among children today, how has this information changed your opinion on the necessity of early identification and treatments for brain imbalances?

SENSORY-MOTOR EXERCISES

Training the Brain Through Physical Stimulation

Key Lessons

1. **Sensory-motor exercises are essential for integrating the body's sensory systems, which include the tactile, vestibular, and proprioceptive systems. These systems collaborate to promote balance, coordination, and spatial awareness, which has a direct impact on a child's capacity to properly interact with their surroundings.**

2. **Neuroplasticity Enhancement: Sensory-motor activities increase brain growth and improve neuroplasticity, the brain's ability to build and restructure synaptic connections, particularly in response to learning or experience or after damage. This is critical for children with neurological problems because it promotes the formation of new brain connections, so assisting in the compensating for impairments in sensory or motor capabilities.**

3. **Improvement in Focus and Attention: Children with ADHD and other neurological diseases can benefit**

considerably from regular participation in structured sensory-motor activities. These activities aid in the modulation of sensory input, which is frequently reported to be difficult for these youngsters, lowering instances of overstimulation and improving their ability to concentrate on tasks.

4. **Strengthening Bilateral Coordination: Sensory-motor activities stress bilateral coordination, or the capacity to use both sides of the body simultaneously. This ability is required for everyday tasks such as walking, running, writing, and other activities that require coordination between limbs, which can be especially difficult for children with neurological diseases.**

5. **Promotion of Emotional and Behavioral Control: Participating in sensory-motor activities relieves stress and can have a substantial influence on emotional and behavioral regulation. These exercises help children with neurological impairments regulate their fear, frustration, and other emotions, leading to more consistent and adaptive behavioral responses.**

Self-Reflection Questions

1. How well do you comprehend the relationship between your sensory experiences and daily activities? Consider how sensory processing may affect your daily activities and interactions.

----

2. Reflect on your experiences learning new physical activities. How can these events affect your brain's ability to adapt and make new connections?

----

3. Consider your capacity to remain focused and attentive during activities. How do you deal with distractions, and may sensory-motor activities help you concentrate?

----

4. Consider how you use both sides of your body in everyday tasks. Are there any places where you see a lack of coordination or difficulties completing activities that need bilateral cooperation?

---

5. **Assess how you presently deal with stress and emotional issues. Could physical activities meant to modulate sensory input help you manage your emotions more effectively?**

NEUROACADEMIC ASSESSMENT AND HOME ACTIVITIES

Aiming for a Better Grade

Key Lessons

1. **The Importance of Personalized Assessments: Understanding each child's own neurological profile is critical. A customized neuroacademic exam can uncover unique strengths and limitations, enabling the creation of specialized home activities that meet individual needs.**

2. **Integrated Learning Strategies: Successful learning requires the integration of sensory, motor, and cognitive capabilities. Home activities that promote integration can improve academic achievement and behavioral outcomes in children with neurological problems.**

3. Consistency and Routine in Practice: Regular, consistent practice of personalized home activities is essential for achieving improvement. Creating a program that combines these activities into your daily life will help reinforce new abilities and behaviors.

4. **Parental Involvement and Support: The involvement of parents and caregivers is critical in the healing process. Active participation, support, and encouragement from parents may significantly improve the efficacy of home activities and the overall learning experience.**

5. **Measuring Progress and Adjusting Strategies: A child's progress must be monitored on a continuous basis. It is critical to frequently examine the success of home activities and make required modifications to techniques to ensure they remain in line with the child's changing requirements.**

Self-Reflection Questions

1. How well do you understand your child's individual neurological and academic strengths and limitations, and how do you use this information to assist their learning and development?

---

2. Do you actively use integrated learning techniques that mix sensory, motor, and cognitive tasks into your child's daily routine to help them flourish academically and socially?

---

3. How consistent are your approaches to implementing prescribed home activities, and what efforts can you take to enhance consistency in order to better support your child's development?

----

4. How actively involved are you, as a parent or caregiver, in your child's learning and therapeutic activities, and how may you increase your engagement and support?

----

5. How regularly do you evaluate the efficacy of your child's home activities, and are you willing to adapt your techniques to match their evolving needs and goals?

WHAT SHOULD 1 FEED MY CHILD?

Brain Balance Nutrition Plan

Key Lessons

1. **The Importance of a Balanced Diet: Emphasize the vital role that a well-balanced diet plays in brain health and function. Nutrients such as omega-3 fatty acids, vitamins, and minerals are required for cognitive development and can impact the behavior and learning capacities of children with neurological diseases.**

2. **Elimination of Processed Food: Highlight the importance of eliminating processed foods from the diet. These meals frequently include chemicals, preservatives, and artificial components, which might impair brain function and increase symptoms of neurological illnesses.**

3. Including Whole Foods: Advocate for a diet high in whole foods, such as fruits, vegetables, lean meats, and whole grains. These meals include critical nutrients and antioxidants that promote brain health and well-being.

4. **Understanding Food Sensitivities: Discuss the significance of recognizing and treating food sensitivities or allergies. Certain meals might cause unfavorable responses in sensitive people, influencing their behavior, mood, and cognitive processes.**

5. **The role of hydration: Emphasize the need of enough water for brain health. Water is required for nutrition transfer, toxin removal, and proper brain function. Encourage the intake of plenty of water throughout the day.**

Self-Reflection Questions

1. **Balanced Diet Reflection: Consider your present diet. Do you consume a wide range of nutrients that promote brain health, such as omega-3 fatty acids, vitamins, and minerals?**

----

2. Processed foods. Evaluate the quantity of processed food you consume on a regular basis. How may decreasing these items and substituting them with full, nutrient-dense alternatives improve your neurological health?

---

3. **Whole Foods Assessment: Evaluate your consumption of whole foods. Are fruits, veggies, lean meats, and whole grains staples in your diet, or might you eat more of them to improve brain health?**

----

4. **Food Sensitivities Consider your physical and emotional sensations after consuming specific meals. Is there anything that routinely causes discomfort or changes in mood or behavior, suggesting a potential sensitivity?**

----

5. **Hydration Check: Think about how much water you drink every day. Are you drinking enough water to keep hydrated and promote optimal brain function and general health?**

HOME BEHAVIOR MODIFICATION PLAN

Getting Back to Normal

Key Lessons

1. **Creating an Organized Environment: The first step toward normalizing behavior and supporting growth in children with neurological problems is to establish a structured environment at home. This entails creating clear and consistent procedures, expectations, and boundaries. A consistent setting lowers anxiety and improves attention, making it simpler for youngsters to learn and practice new actions.**

2. **Positive Reinforcement Techniques: Use positive reinforcement to encourage desired actions. Recognizing and praising positive acts and accomplishments, no matter how tiny, reinforces their importance to the kid and encourages recurrence. This strategy focuses on promoting good acts rather than addressing poor behavior.**

3. **Customized Activities for Skill Development:** Involve children in activities that are tailored to their unique needs and abilities. These activities should try to strengthen areas of difficulty, such as social skills, coordination, or intellectual ability, while also focusing on the child's strengths. Personalized activities guarantee that the youngster is neither over- or under-stimulated.

4. **Family Involvement and Support:** Healing and progress work best in a supportive family atmosphere. Encourage all family members to engage in the child's development plan, creating a continuous support structure that encourages feelings of security and belonging. This collaborative effort helps to normalize behavioral alteration as a part of daily living.

5. **Regular Monitoring and Adjustment:** Continue to monitor the child's progress and the efficacy of the home behavior modification strategy. Prepare to alter techniques as the child's needs evolve. This adaptive method keeps the strategy current and effective, encouraging ongoing development and progress.

Self-Reflection Questions

1. How effective is your present home structure in providing your child with a predictable environment? Consider how routines, expectations, and limits are set and maintained.

----

2. How do you now employ positive reinforcement to support your child's desirable actions, and how may you improve these practices to foster even more positive development?

---

3. Consider the tailored activities you've created for your youngster. Are they designed to both challenge and use your child's individual talents and needs?

----

4. Determine the extent of family engagement in your child's development plan. How can you increase family support and engagement to provide a more caring and cohesive environment for your child?

----

5. Consider the last time you assessed the efficacy of your home behavior modification program. How frequently do you review your child's growth, and what criteria do you use to determine whether changes are necessary?

SELF-EVALUATION QUESTIONS

1. How has your knowledge of neurological illnesses such as autism, ADHD, dyslexia, and others altered since completing this workbook? Think about any previous assumptions you had and how your perspective has changed.

---

2. How have you used the Brain Balance Program's ideas and procedures at home? Consider the precise methods or activities you've employed and their effects on your child's behavior and growth.

---

3. What difficulties did you have when implementing the themes from "Disconnected Kids" in your daily life? Consider the challenges you faced and how you adapted or overcome them.

----

4. How has your attitude to managing and supporting your child's neurological disease changed since the beginning of this workbook? Identify any substantial shifts in your behavior, attitudes, or expectations.

----

5. What accomplishments or gains have you seen in your child's social, intellectual, or behavioral skills as a consequence of using the Brain Balance Program? Make a note of the areas where development was most obvious.

----

6. Consider how family engagement and support have influenced your child's development. How have you and other family members helped to foster a supportive and loving atmosphere for growth?

---

7. What are your next actions in supporting your child's development with the ideas and practices from "Disconnected Kids"? Identify any areas that you believe require extra emphasis or adaption.

A Special Note of Thanks

Dear Esteemed Reader,

As the pages of this book unfold, so does the story of a journey—a journey not just of the author, but one that we have embarked on together. Your decision to invest your time and open your heart to the words within these covers has contributed to a shared narrative of discovery, learning, and growth.

Gratitude for Your Presence

Your presence in this journey is a gift beyond measure. It is you, the reader, who transforms ink on paper into vivid landscapes of thought, emotion, and action. The lifeblood of this book is not just the stories it tells but the conversations it starts, the ideas it sparks, and the connections it fosters.

The Essence of Our Shared Journey

This book is a testament to the power of stories to unite us, challenge us, and inspire us to see the world through a broader lens. Each chapter was crafted with the hope of offering not just insights but also a space for reflection and personal growth. Your engagement with this work enriches its meaning and extends its reach beyond the confines of its pages.

Looking to the Horizon

As we look ahead, the journey does not end here. The conversations that begin in these pages are meant to continue, to ripple out into our lives and communities. Your reflections, insights, and stories are invaluable as we navigate this path forward, exploring new ideas and forging new connections.

An Invitation

While this note marks a pause in our shared narrative, it is by no means a conclusion. I invite you to carry the spirit of this journey forward, in whatever form resonates with you. Whether through discussions with friends, reflections shared online, or moments of personal contemplation, your experiences with this book are a powerful force for growth and connection.

With Deepest Appreciation

Thank you for being a part of this journey. Your presence, from the first page to the last, has been a source of encouragement and inspiration. As we each move forward, I carry with me the hope that the stories and insights shared within these pages will continue to resonate and inspire.

Until our paths cross again in the pages of another adventure,

Heath print

heathprintco@gmail.com you can always reach out to us on here. Thanks.

Made in the USA
Coppell, TX
06 June 2025

50417310R00059